About Adoration

by

STEVE MANSON

Disclaimer

This Book is claimed and composed by Professor Steve Manson, who is otherwise called the writer of the book.

Book Review

About Adoration is a book written by Professor Steve Manson which tells more about adoration, love affection and feelings and how it can be be influencial to us.

TABLE OF CONTENT

Part 1: Significance of Affection

Love is an intense word to make sense of, and the importance of adoration? That gets more mind-boggling and basic simultaneously!

"We need to understand what love is, I believe that you should show me." Indeed, a band of men with extremely terrible hair sang those definite words. Indeed, even now, such a long time later, we're actually requesting ourselves what the genuine definition of affection is.

What does it really closely resemble? Indeed, the word reference characterizes it, however, it's not exactly to the point of making sense of the staggering surge of feelings that we feel, right?

What is the genuine importance of affection? What's more, for what reason does everybody characterize it in an unexpected way? Truly, however, the

explanation? Since it's different for everyone who encounters it.
What is the genuine importance of adoration, and what's the significance here?
Making sense of adoration is like attempting to make sense of why water is wet - it simply is! There are various types of affection - heartfelt love, family love, companionship love, and love you have for the things you do. Each and every sort of adoration is legitimate and genuine for you.
It's not outside the realm of possibilities that you experience it another way with another person in your life. All of us are remarkable and that implies we perceive insight, and sense loves in somewhat diverse ways as well.
Notwithstanding, there is some shared belief finally. The genuine importance of

affection is very foggy, yet many individuals put it down as:

1. The capacity to comprehend and acknowledge someone else as they are, totally
2. Needing the absolute best for an individual and assisting them with being their best selves they can be
3. Assuming it came down to it, you'd forfeit your own bliss for theirs
4. Needing to fabricate a future with that individual
5. At any rate, seeing the great and terrible pieces of somebody and adoring them
6. A profound association and a sensation of being entire.

As may be obvious, the genuine significance of adoration is boundless and you could have an alternate thought of what it is to you.

For the vast majority, in any case, the above assertions sound valid. You believe the best for that individual and disdain should see them battling or enduring, and you'd forfeit your own bliss to guarantee that they're grinning.

Love in the entirety of its sorts has these definitions, whether we're discussing family, companions, or heartfelt love. At the point when we love a person or thing, we need it in our lives and become connected to it, to the place where being without it is excruciating.

Part 2:
Kinds of Affection

8 Unique Kinds of Adoration

What various sorts of adoration would you say you are right now encountering and how can they influence your life?

1. "Eros" or Suggestive Love

The main sort of adoration is Eros, which is named after the Greek divine force of affection and fruitfulness. Eros addresses the possibility of sexual energy and want. The old Greeks believed Eros to be perilous and startling as it includes a "deficiency of control" through the basic drive to reproduce. Eros is an enthusiastic and serious type of adoration that excites heartfelt and sexual sentiments.

Eros is a gloried and delightfully optimistic love that in the hearts of the profoundly stirred can be utilized to "review information on excellence" (as

Socrates put it) through Tantra and otherworldly sex. Be that as it may, when misinformed, eros can be abused, manhandled, and enjoyed, prompting rash demonstrations and broken hearts.

Eros is a base and strong fire that wears out rapidly. It needs its fire to be fanned through one of the more deeply types of affection underneath as it is revolved around the self-centered parts of adoration, that is to say, individual fascination and actual joy.

2. "Philia" or Warm Love

The second sort of adoration is philia or fellowship. The old Greeks esteemed philia far above eros since it was viewed as an adoration between rises.

Plato felt that actual fascination was not an essential piece of adoration, thus the utilization of the word dispassionate implies, "without actual fascination." Philia is a sort of adoration that is felt among companions who've persevered through difficult situations together.

philia is an "impartial temperate love" that is liberated from the power of physical allure. It frequently includes the sensations of faithfulness among companions, kinship among partners, and the feeling of penance for your

3. "Storage" or Natural Love

In spite of the fact that storage intently looks like philia in that it is affection without actual fascination, storage is fundamentally to do with connection and commonality. Storage is a characteristic type of love that frequently streams among guardians and their kids, and youngsters for their folks.

Storge love could actually be found among cherished companions that are subsequently shared as grown-ups. Be that as it may, despite the fact that storage is a strong type of affection, it can likewise turn into a hindrance to our otherworldly ways, particularly when our family or companions don't line up with or support our excursion.

4. "Ludus" or Lively Love

In spite of the fact that Ludus has a touch of sensual eros in it, it is considerably more than that. The Greeks considered Ludus as an energetic type of affection, for instance, the friendship between youthful sweethearts.

Ludus is that feeling we have when we go through the beginning phases of falling head over heels for somebody, for example, the shuddering heart, being a tease, prodding, and sensations of rapture.

Energy in adoration is a fundamental fixing that is many times lost in long-haul connections. However, liveliness is one of the keys to keeping the honest guiltlessness of your adoration alive, fascinating, and invigorating.

5. "Madness" or Over the top Love

Insanity love is a sort of adoration that drives an accomplice into a kind of franticness and obsessiveness. It happens when there is an irregularity between eros and Ludus.

To the people who experience lunacy, love itself is a method for saving themselves; a support of their own worth as the victim of unfortunate confidence. This individual needs to cherish and be wanted to discover healthy identity esteem. Along these lines, they can become possessive and envious sweethearts, feeling like they frantically "need" their accomplices.

On the off chance that the other accomplice neglects to respond with a similar sort of insanity love, many issues win. To this end, craziness can frequently prompt issues like codependency

6. "Pragma" or Persevering through Adoration

Pragma is an affection that has matured, developed, and been created over the long run. It is past the physical, it has risen above the relaxed, and a one-of-a-kind congruity has framed after some time.

You can find pragma in wedded couples who've been together for quite a while, or in kinships that have persevered for a really long time. Sadly pragma is a sort of adoration that isn't effortlessly found. We invest such a lot of significant investment attempting to track down adoration thus a brief period in figuring out how to keep up with it.

In contrast to different sorts of affection, pragma is the aftereffect of exertion on the two sides. It's the affection between individuals who've figured out how to make splits the difference, and have exhibited persistence and resilience to make the relationship.

7. "Philautia" or Confidence

The Greeks comprehended that to really focus on others, we should initially figure out how to really focus on ourselves. This type of self-esteem isn't the undesirable vanity and self-fixation that is centered around private notoriety, gain and fortune similarly to Self-absorption.

All things being equal, philautia is confident in its best structure. It shares the Buddhist way of thinking of "self-sympathy" which is the profound comprehension that just once you have the solidarity to cherish yourself and feel content just being yourself, can you give love to other people. As Aristotle put it, "All accommodating affections for others are an expansion of a man's affections for himself."

You can't share what you don't have. In the event that you don't cherish yourself, you can't adore any other person by the same token. The best way to really be blissful is to track down that unqualified love for yourself. Frequently figuring out how to adore yourself includes embracing every one of the characteristics you see as "repulsive", this is where shadow work comes in.

8. "Agape" or Caring Adoration

The most noteworthy and most extreme kind of adoration as indicated by the Greeks is agape or sacrificial genuine love.

This sort of affection isn't the nostalgic overflow that frequently passes as adoration in our general public. It doesn't have anything to do with the condition-based kind of affection that our sex-fixated culture attempts to pass as adoration.

Agape some call otherworldly love. It is an unrestricted love, greater than ourselves, an unfathomable sympathy, and endless compassion. The Buddhists portray it as "mettā" or "all-inclusive adoring benevolence." the most perfect type of affection is liberated from wants and assumptions, and loves no matter what the blemishes and weaknesses of others.

Agape is the adoration that is felt for that which we instinctively know as the heavenly truth: the affection that acknowledges, pardons, and accepts our more noteworthy great.

Part 3:
Justifications for why love falls flat?

1. Loss of Trust

One of the primary sentiments important in a decent relationship is a sense of safety. On the off chance that you need consistent encouragement or find your accomplice inconsistent, you could lose trust.

Assuming your accomplice is unclear or difficult to nail down, there is reason to worry. Connections that are based on the question are in dangerous territory.

2. Lying

Suppose you figured out your accomplice deceived you. Untruths can have strong outcomes. Was it an innocent embellishment or a falsehood told to safeguard the individual who lied? Harmless exaggerations are many times minor or irrelevant while genuine falsehoods have expansive impacts.

3. Possessiveness

On the off chance that you're with an excessively possessive, accomplice, ask yourself, "Does this appear to be solid? Does your accomplice segregate you away from your companions or continually investigate you?"

4. Jealousy

Envy in little dosages can be solid and a sign that you're not underestimating each other. Be that as it may, in the event that somebody is excessively possessive and appears to display indications of obsessive envy, these are warnings.

5. Poor Correspondence

Assuming that you're both diminished to just talking about the children's timetables or the errand list for the end of the week, your correspondence has become simply value-based. Sound interchanges ought to be about loads of various points.

6. Infidelity

In the event that you suspect your accomplice is being faithless, you might feel like the foundation of what you constructed together has been annihilated. You probably won't confide in this individual any longer. Is it true that they are even who you thought they were?

Connections focused on the absence of trust, loaded up with lying, desire, and disloyalty, will probably not persevere.

Part 4:
Can genuine romance endure anything?

Genuine romance loves you, yet it always remembers to adore itself. It generally needs to be solid in whole self to give you a better and more grounded relationship. Then again, counterfeit love couldn't care less about its own government assistance. It childishly harms itself for the purpose of implosion, giving you more agony and issues your relationship doesn't merit. Genuine affection generally looks for self-awareness and development in your relationship. It fills in as a good example. It generally rouses and propels you to be a superior individual. Then again, counterfeit love loves battling and warmed contentions. It doesn't have the foggiest idea of how to tranquilly settle things. It toxifies your relationship and obliterates your great life.

Genuine affection isn't simply all discussion and commitments. It's not even about simple activities. Genuine romance demonstrations with enthusiasm, fervor, and energy. It generally needs awesome for you. It is reluctant to let you down. Then again, counterfeit love is casual towards you. It generally leaves you with pardons as opposed to satisfying its commitments to you. True love remembers you for its future and sees you as an individual it needs to be with until the end of its life. For that reason, it never quits any pretense of battling for yourself as well as your relationship. Then again, counterfeit love has no long-lasting designs for you. Hence, it doesn't regard you as significant, and it effectively abandons you.

Genuine affection depends on and has confidence in you in spite of your shortcomings and deficiencies. Then again, counterfeit love needs to have 100 percent confirmation that you are reliable prior to depending on or trusting in you.

Part 5:
Could everybody at any point love

Love can have numerous implications (from affection for a youngster as their parent to heartfelt love). In all cases, however, love implies feeling sympathy and empathy for another being past basic friendship.

Furthermore, the miserable response is, that there are individuals who can't have this inclination. In severe mental terms, they have total disregard for other people. In layman's terms, they are sociopaths and mental cases. What portrays these individuals is a failure to feel sympathy for other people and in this manner, powerlessness to feel genuine romance (they might have short-lived sensations of fondness or association, however, determined by personal circumstance).

Indeed, this kind of trouble in adulthood can begin in youth with profound disregard.

It isn't so much that nobody really likes or loves you. I'm certain there are individuals who do. The issue is that as a result of your young life experience, you have a lot of trouble trusting it.

It then, at that point, turns into an inevitable outcome. Your trust issues keep you from answering individuals' fondness and love as they expect; they botch that for indifference and ended up floating away from you.

So this is the sort of endless loop I figure you might be caught in.

The past can't be changed. Assuming you actually need time to lament what you missed in adolescence, take that time. It's significant. However, at that point set the previous aside among your

recollections and begin dealing with fixing the issue that exists on the spot.
The fact that little youngster is additional makes you not. You're an experienced grown-up and completely engaged to assume responsibility for your life, companionships, and connections. Assuming that trust issues are the issue, these can be fixed. Yet, you really want to take that first, hardest step alone: to connect with the expert to assist you with requiring.
At the point when you love whatever or whomever you truly do mentally really benefit. It is actually straightforward. Love - communicating it - doing it - spreading it is benefiting. You can cherish a specific bloom and each time you see it you feel like your heart opens up. That is beneficial for you at that time. In any event, when the second is simply 20 seconds long.

What you are requesting is uneven love - yes we can profit from uneven love until we hope to be adored back and this doesn't occur. Then the enduring kicks in. Yet, the enduring isn't established in affection it is attached to the assumption to be cherished back. Consequently, you won't ever have an issue when you love a specific bloom, since there is no assumption on the planet that this one loves you back.

Thus you truly do have a more modest gathering who experienced in their adoration existence with others pulling out from the human love and proceeding to protest love.

In any case, love - we as a whole generally benefit from it. There is absolutely no chance of not doing such.

www.ingramcontent.com/pod-product-compliance
Lightning Source LLC
LaVergne TN
LVHW020544160826
845677LV00015B/4201
9798353334859